A Peace That Passes All
UNDERSTANDING

One Man's Journey
after the Suicide of his Son

JIM RANNELLS

WESTBOW
PRESS®
A DIVISION OF THOMAS NELSON
& ZONDERVAN

Scripture taken from the New King James Version®. Copyright © 1982 by Thomas Nelson. Used by permission. All rights reserved.

Scripture quotations marked (NLT) are taken from the Holy Bible, New Living Translation, copyright © 1996, 2004, 2007 by Tyndale House Foundation. Used by permission of Tyndale House Publishers, Inc., Carol Stream, Illinois 60188. All rights reserved.

The Living Bible copyright © 1971 by Tyndale House Foundation. Used by permission of Tyndale House Publishers Inc., Carol Stream, Illinois 60188. All rights reserved. The Living Bible, TLB, and the The Living Bible logo are registered trademarks of Tyndale House Publishers.

NEW LIFE Version © Christian Literature International. Christian Literature International (CLI) is a non-profit ministry dedicated to publishing and providing the Word of God in a form that can be read and understood by new readers and the well-educated alike... and at an affordable price. We invite you to learn how the NEW LIFE Version unlocks the treasures of God's Word!

WestBow Press books may be ordered through booksellers or by contacting:

WestBow Press
A Division of Thomas Nelson & Zondervan
1663 Liberty Drive
Bloomington, IN 47403
www.westbowpress.com
1 (866) 928-1240

ISBN: 978-1-9736-0725-0 (sc)
ISBN: 978-1-9736-0724-3 (e)

Library of Congress Control Number: 2017917301

Print information available on the last page.

WestBow Press rev. date: 11/10/2017

Contents

Foreword vii

Introduction ix

Chapter 1   Hitting the Very Bottom in My Life 1
Chapter 2   Running Away 5
Chapter 3   Finding the Start of Peace 9
Chapter 4   More of This Peace 15
Chapter 5   All Things Do Work Together 25
Chapter 6   Peace through God's Restoration 29
Chapter 7   Peace in Life versus Death 33
Chapter 8   Peace over Our Children 35
Chapter 9   Peace through a Resistance to the Conformity of
            the World 39
Chapter 10 Peace through Forgiveness 43
Chapter 11 Peace Despite Politics 47
Chapter 12 Suicide (or the Lack of Hope as the Cause) 53
Chapter 13 Peace of God versus Peace with God 57
Chapter 14 Peace in Our Health 59
Chapter 15 Trusting in the Sovereignty of God 61

Conclusion 65

Foreword

The realization that God is in control is how I would sum up this peace I have found. Really, it's a recognition of the fact that we can align ourselves with this control of God or go our own way in disobedience, just like we did before we accepted Christ as our Savior. When we turn our lives over to Christ, nothing happens that God doesn't pre-ordain. He sees the bigger picture and uses our trials in life for us to gain even more faith in Him through Christ. This ultimately transforms into a trust in God. I would say gaining a trust in God and receiving the peace of God are synonymous, or the two facets work hand in hand.

As a Christian believer, when I look back at my life, I can see the sovereignty of God working though my past and present trials in order to bring me to this trust in Him. Ultimately, He wanted me to write about this peace that I have found. I realize that He brings me though lessons in life that ultimately make my faith more solid. I can honestly agree with the notion the Paul writes about in Romans: "All things work together for the good of those who love God."

Yes, I have denied God a lot and gone my own way in my free will. But even then, Christ has brought me to a place where I trust His provisions of my faith more fully.

It is my prayer that readers of this book can find the trust in God as I have found, along with that blessed peace that passes all understanding. Readers can also learn how to preserve that peace, because the world we live in has many ways in which it can rob us of that peace. We should at least recognize those things that may rob us of our peace, and we should know where to go to find answers.

In my testimony, which is this book, I try to point out the many ways I have found to preserve that peace now that I've found it. The world (through Satan) has many ways in which we can be robbed of that peace. I attempt to show how we can preserve the peace that passes all understanding.

Introduction

I felt the need to put in a background of sorts as to the event that totally changed my life and brought me on the pathway where I was to become a new creation in Christ. I also want to show how utterly selfish I was for the first forty-five years of my life. Then Christ rescued me through His peace that passes all understanding, and He guarded my heart and mind, as listed in Philippians 4:7.

At the onset of this book, I want to point to Christ from the very first, because it is about Him and what He accomplished in my life. I am simply the recipient of His grace.

I could sum up those first forty-five years of my life as a selfish, rebelling jerk. I was selfish because mostly I thought only of myself and less on the feelings of others. Certainly, I thought less on the consequences of my own actions. I simply did not care most of the time. I also had a rebelling nature, because I rebelled from my own father and the false church in which I was brought up. The only problem is that I took that rebelling nature to the extreme.

Calling myself a jerk is somewhat self-explanatory, and when I reflect on what motivated me in the past, with all the selfishness and all the rebelling against God, *jerk* describes me well.

This is not to say that now in Christ, my flesh does not get the better of me at times. But a faith in Christ is what I and all who claim a belief in Christ have, and we strive to live in the Spirit more fully.

I spent all of my childhood and high school years as an obedient son to a dad who deeply desired for me to eventually take over our family's cattle ranch in Wyoming, which had been in our family for five generations. My great, great grandfather cleared the sagebrush from the land and bought it from the Indians in the mid-1800s. I was the only son in my generation, but I knew early on that this ranching life was not for me. I did my best to somewhat try to please my father until I met the goal of getting out on my own by going to college.

This brought on many conflicts with my dad, as well as with my mother, who brought up my four sisters and me up following the Mormon religion. I think early on, when I was in my teen years, I knew something was wrong with that religion, even if I could not quite put my finger on why I had problems with it. It would take many years to discover why it was wrong and why I would eventually deny that religion, which on my mother's side went back five generations to the times of Brigham Young.

When I left for college in 1969, I started a life rebellion against my father and the Mormon Church. I learned to drink and party, and I started many years of womanizing. As I said, the drinking was my way of proving I was a Jack Mormon, and I think I formally drank to that aspect many times. Occasionally at college, I even managed the time to study, and I chose a major in music because I liked to sing in high school and could actually sing on key.

After a couple of years of college with a lot of drinking, I met a woman and got her pregnant. We married a few months before my daughter, Amber, was born. My new wife, Kim, and I both left college, and I perused a job in restaurant management to support my new family. The problem was I was not mature enough to stop my rebelling, and I was soon back to my drinking and womanizing outside our marriage. Kim and I divorced after about three years, and I drifted from job to job for a while. I did not take full responsibility for my young daughter until the courts caught up with me a few years later due to all the back child support I had accumulated. I was still a selfish, rebelling jerk—with the addition of a lack of responsibility for my young daughter.

A couple of years later, I met my next wife, Darlene, and we ended up having two children together. I think I then gained a bit more responsibility in that marriage, although we ended up aborting what would have been our third child in 1978 because we thought we couldn't afford another child. I believe that foolish decision we made led to a lot of problems between us. We ended up separating and then sharing the two children for the next six years, until we both started to mature and tried to make our marriage work once again. That maturing process was definitely aided by our involvement in the Methodist Church, where I was asked to sing in their choir. It got us going to church every Sunday. I think both Darlene and I realized something was missing in our lives and in our marriage, and faith in God seemed to be the key.

But our growing together and learning about God was to be cut short by her untimely death in 1987 in a car accident. I suppose I was angry at God for taking my wife when we had started to find a way to better our marriage. As things were starting to get better, I was suddenly faced with an emptiness by her death. But as I learned later, it was another lesson in my life that I sorely needed.

Darlene liked to do what she referred to as "letting her hair down," and she still partied on rare occasions. One night in late October 1987, she and a friend went out partying at bars after leaving both sets of children with a babysitter; I was at work that evening. The two ended up driving along a long stretch of road where they had a single-car rollover. My wife was ejected from the car, broke her neck, and died instantly, according to the coroner. The other woman ended up with only minor injuries, and there were no witnesses to the actual accident. The highway patrolman who investigated that accident concluded that my wife was driving. I must accept his conclusions, even though there may have been more partial evidence presented to me after the fact to possibly dispute his findings. Sometimes things are not quite so clear in our lives, and then we feel we must resort to our opinions when questions remain.

I was approximately eight miles away from the accident scene after getting off work. God moved me to drive down that particular highway, not knowing what I would find. I came upon the wrecked car and my wife lying on the shoulder of the road. In the need to do something, I tried to administer CPR to her for an undetermined length of time, until the highway patrolman put his hand on my shoulder and said, "It's too late," confirming what I already knew deep inside. Later that night, after I went home and told our two children what had happened with their mother, it was a unique bonding moment for us. Our children were ten and eleven when their mother died. I believe I developed a deep resolve to do my best as a single father, for what turned out to be a three-year mourning period for myself.

Loneliness eventually got the better of me, and I started answering newspaper and magazine dating ads. God certainly was not a part of my decision to find a new wife, and I eventually met and married a woman who lived clear across the country in New Hampshire. I moved her and her youngest daughter out to Wyoming. Her daughter went to high school here, along with my two children. I was laid off from my job a year later here in Wyoming, and eventually we all moved to New Hampshire, where I took on an OTR trucking job. This marriage did not last because our differences were quite severe, so my children and I moved back to Wyoming after a year and a half of living in New Hampshire. In my stubbornness, I would not give up on that marriage, and I once again moved her back to Wyoming, where we remarried. Thankfully for both of us, she moved down to Colorado to live with her daughter, and we eventually divorced for the final time. I simply did not seek God's guidance before I asked her to marry me either time.

During this period after my wife's death, I had many wonderful Christians plant many seeds in me and my two children. One wonderful Christian woman took both my children under her wing and got them involved with a Southern Baptist church. They both went to the church's summer camp, and both were saved at that camp. They went there for three summers.

I sang in the Methodist church choir, along with singing in a multi-church choir led by a wonderful Christian man who recently passed away. The music I was singing in those many years planted seeds in me. One wonderful Christian woman asked me to sing in her fun band, as it was called. She would play the piano while I and a couple of others would lead the nursing home residents in many Christian hymns. This woman was instrumental in me eventually joining the Baptist church of which I am now a member, and I have been for sixteen years.

In 1994, I started going to a Church of God denomination because a man I worked with was the pastor there. He and his church established more questions as to my Mormon religion, which was very much a part of me for some forty-odd years and which I had yet to deny. The true Christ was being presented to me in this church and in the Methodist church, so I was still on the outside looking in as to receiving the true Christ until I was to later reject the Mormon Christ in favor of the biblical Christ.

Then in January 1995, I was back to drinking a bit more and felt God calling me to admit myself into a Christian counseling center in California.

I had picked up a Christian publication handout in the entrance of the church I was going to at the time. I took it home and felt led to call the number listed for the counseling center. I found out that my work's group insurance would pay for all but two hundred dollars for this two-week stay. My two children were seventeen and eighteen at the time, and so I left them in the care of my sister and my parents, who lived nearby. I flew down to Anaheim, California, for this counseling stay. It was to be another step in the process where God was to prepare me for what would transpire just four months later. That brings me to the start of my book.

1

Hitting the Very Bottom in My Life

When someone becomes a Christian, he becomes a brand-new
person inside. He is not the same anymore. A new life has begun!

—2 Corinthians 5:17 (TLB)

That early summer day in 1995 started out like most. There was nice sunshine, and I had some work to do in my garden. I had agreed to work with my son, Larry, later that morning rebuilding the carburetor on his car. His first car was a big ol' boat in the form of a 1982 Dodge station wagon; he had even added a coat of wax onto its fading finish. Fixing that car up to be roadworthy was a part in his plans to go off to a trade school in Phoenix, Arizona, later that summer, where he and his friend were moving. The two boys had already taken a trip down there the month before to check out apartments, the schools they would attend, and even places to find part-time work. They both had their plans formulated, along with the funding to start their educations and live in Phoenix. I had helped Larry with a big deposit for the first semester of his trade school, and I planned to continue helping him achieve his goals.

Larry had finally found his niche in life, and his aptitudes were in computer technology. Even though it was the mid-nineties at that time, and we were still somewhat in the pre-Internet age, he had already taken apart and put back together our small, personal Atari computer several times. Larry was clearly in his element when it came to computers. Even when he was in high school, a couple of teachers had assured me that he could go very far in that field because they too saw an excitement in him with this technology. It was a new life of learning before him in a field that fascinated him. The technology has advanced so much since then, and I could see him now working for some software company designing some program, or even designing hardware. He was fascinated by new technology. I was so excited for him and was proud that he was finally formulating some solid goals in a field in which I knew he would succeed. I never would have guessed what was to transpire later that morning.

When he got up that morning and made himself breakfast, I asked him about some VCR tapes (certainly some readers will remember that technology) that he had agreed to copy for people at our church. That question soon turned into an argument, and he left the kitchen, stormed to his room, and locked himself inside. He was my only son, and given the fact that we were so similar in our demeanor, I knew we would both eventually cool down and apologize to each other. I knew he had a handgun, but suicide was not on my mind.

An hour or so later, I went to his bedroom door and asked through the door, "We okay, son?"

What ensued next was something I heard and then instinctively knew. A large-caliber pistol going off in a closed room is very distinctive, and for most all of us, we must investigate to confirm, even if what we want to confirm could potentially be horrifying or deadly. My own need to visually confirm what I thought to be true was certainly there in me at that very moment. After breaking through his locked bedroom door, I gained a picture in my mind that will never be erased.

It is true that time stands still for significant moments in our lives. A second can seem to last an eternity when, from one monumental experience, a torrent of separate emotions comes into our minds. I do not think I could fully describe what a pistol to the head does when it is fired, with the traumatic carnage from a bullet entering and leaving the skull— coupled with the fact that this was my own flesh and blood who was sitting there on his bed. I don't think there was a single negative human emotion absent in me in that very moment, including a violent, physical revulsion. My picture in my mind that morning was one of physical sickness and deep horror, and certainly the ugliness of death. Now, with a more completed, spiritual view, that picture includes so much deep joy and peace, because Christ with outstretched arms is standing in that picture. This story has a happy, joyful ending, so I encourage the reader to read on. From my tragedy, I found the peace that passes all understanding, and my trust in God is more solid. It is my deep desire to continue to learn of Him.

2

Running Away

But Jonah ran away from the Lord going toward Tarshish.
He went down to Joppa and found a ship which was
going to Tarshish. Jonah paid money, and got on the
ship to go with them, to get away from the Lord.

—Jonah 1:3 (NLV)

Running away and trying to hide from it all was my first reaction after I took in the whole scene. It is in our human nature to run away from that which horrifies or is any sort of a problem we cannot handle. It is part of our nature to run away from the Lord when facing our problems, like Jonah did from God's direction, as we read in the verse above. Certainly, I was initially running away from God because I didn't want to hold on to that horrifying picture of my son in that moment. Neither did I want to face the fact that as his father, I had not seen the signs beforehand of his suicide. There were a lot of whys and much self-blame in my running and hiding. I was simply running away and then running toward what was familiar to me: an alcohol solution to drown it all out in my mind.

And they heard the sound of the LORD God walking
in the garden in the cool of the day, and Adam and his
wife hid themselves from the presence of the LORD God
among the trees of the garden. (Genesis 3:8)

Adam and Eve clearly tried to hide from God the fact that they had disobeyed Him—and that Satan had deceived them. They tried to hide knowing good and evil and the fact that they had clearly disobeyed God's instruction to not eat of the fruit of the tree of the knowledge of good and evil caused them to hide from Him. That is, until God confronted them.

What I was doing in my running away was attempting to hide myself through running to an alcohol solution once again. I couldn't face God with the fact that I had failed as a father and hadn't protected that son He had given me to care for after his mother's death. I had tried to protect my son from bullying at school years before, and I had tried to help him get over his mother's death. However, I failed miserably that day he took his life. And I failed his sister as well, who was certainly a part of our bonding as a family. Thankfully, she was away in another town that day, so at least she was protected from what I saw. The blame was solely on myself regarding what had happened.

The other big thing I was running away from was the big question: Where did my son go after his death? Like many, I had heard that heaven was no place for those who took their own lives. The religion I grew up in made it very clear that suicide was a major sin and that God dealt harshly with those who took their own lives. This question ran through my mind, along with my own deep guilt. For a few short moments, I was starting to suffer a major breakdown because of the horror I had just witnessed.

God does things at times in an obvious, visual manner, as He did for me that day. I didn't realize until months later how simple it was that He stopped me from my running. After seeing my son in death, I ran up from his basement bedroom to the front of the house and toward my car. I conceivably might have gone to a bar for a big bottle of whiskey. But then God caused me to trip over the base of my wood stove, which was made from bricks. I hit my head, got a tiny gash there, and was effectively stopped in my running. When I got up from my fall, I was dazed a tiny bit from hitting my head on those bricks, and the alcohol solution was no longer a desire. I started to feel a sense of comfort or peace. This was the very first time I'd received the peace that passes all understanding.

I then uttered a very basic, pleading prayer. "God, help me." It was a simple prayer where I was in total humility before Him to receive His grace through Jesus Christ, which is all it takes for any of us, as this verse attests to.

But He Therefore He says: "God resists the proud, but *gives grace to the humble.*" (James 4:6, emphasis mine)

I think my faith in that moment was a tiny mustard seed that was more in line with a hope that God would help me. And as it turned out, He did, even with my faith that was far from complete. I believe I was like the man who asked Jesus to cast out the demon possessing his son (Mark 8:17–26). I too essentially asked, "Lord, I believe, help my unbelief!" (Mark 8:24).

Really, that is all it takes for any one of us: a total and complete humbleness before Christ, who will give us the grace to overcome every situation in our lives, no matter how big or how small. I was to learn much more of this solid promise. My faith in Christ has grown these past twenty-two years. No fancy prayers, but an honest pleading for Him to come into our lives with complete and total humbleness before God through Jesus Christ.

I also came upon these verses early on in my journey to find this peace.

> Come to Me, all you who labor and are heavy laden, and I will give you rest. Take My yoke upon you and learn from Me, for I am gentle and lowly in heart, and you will find rest for your souls. For My yoke is easy and My burden is light. (Matthew 11:28–30)

My burden was more than I could bear, and I knew that I could not face it on my own. My humble prayer was beginning to be answered at that very moment of "God, help me." These words from Jesus suggest a deep peacefulness in trusting in Him. Turning to Him suggests a strong tower of sorts, which lines up with this notion.

> That is why he provided Israel with cities were set aside so that any Israelite who had overwhelming "unawares" by a problem could "run unto one of these cities that he might live." (Deuteronomy 4:42)

Today we have something even better. God has provided us with a strong tower to which we can run and be helped in times of need.

"The Name of the Lord is a strong tower: the righteous run into it, and is safe." (Proverbs 18:10)

David in times of trouble, fled to the Rock. Jesus invites us to run under the shelter of his wings. When many of His disciples were forsaking Him, Jesus turned to the twelve and asked, "Will you run away too, like the others?" Peter answered Him, "Lord, to whom shall we go? Thou hast the words of eternal life." Peter was convinced that Jesus was the only place to hide—the only place to rest. (Excerpts for David Wilkerson's Sermon, "Why Not Just Run Away from It All?")

In my case, where I was at first likely running to was toward an alcohol solution—the desire to buy a big bottle of whiskey so that, from my so-called answers in the past, I could try to bury my memory that I had just established. It was a temptation to go toward what has partially worked in my past and what I was familiar with: getting drunk for me, staying that way, and likely have a big repressed memory in my mind—if I didn't die from alcohol poisoning or liver disease first. That was my preferred, time-tested imitation solution that I, like so many, have gained in our established, worldly solutions: to not face our problems. It is all is running from the Lord and His perfect solutions.

As I mentioned earlier, part of my running away from God was over the abortion my wife, Darlene, and I had had in 1978. It's something I tried to avoid in myself, and for those who have ever gone through it all, whether being a father or a mother to an aborted child, the underlying guilt truly never leaves us until we find the forgiveness through Christ for such a foolish, selfish act.

3

Finding the Start of Peace

And the peace of God, which surpasses all understanding,
will guard your hearts and minds through Christ Jesus.

—Philippians 4:7

In the years since, I have looked to many sources to gain a clearer understanding of what I experienced that day. It is our human nature to sometimes dismiss things that are clearly of Christ, and maybe we do not recognize the complete gravity of a situation. We sometimes try to explain it all as mere chance. But Christ can be in all facets of our lives, even before we come to a solid faith in Him, as my experience clearly indicated to me. All it took for me was a complete humbleness before Him with complete submission to Him, as I later more fully established. I discovered I had a form of post-traumatic stress disorder for a few moments, before Christ rescued me.

According to PsychGuides.com, "PTSD is generally caused by personally experiencing or witnessing a traumatic event. This can include a single event such as a serious accident, assault or sudden death of a loved one."

It clearly was a form of PTSD that I experienced, and there was nothing that indicated a strength in me to have seen my own flesh and blood in death and then be able to handle that trauma, as well as all the guilt and questions over my son's eternal destiny. It has become so clear to me that it was all about Christ from that moment forward and how He clearly saved me from that moment onward. The stress was simply too big to have handled it on my own.

"The level of stress that a person feels after losing a loved one to suicide is catastrophically high—equivalent to that of a highly traumatic concentration camp experience," according to the American Psychiatric Association's "Diagnostic and Statistical Manual of Mental Disorders."

> In other words, if we established a "stress scale" from 0 to 100, with 100 being the highest, losing a loved one to suicide would rank at 100 – the highest stress level imaginable. (Kevin Caruso, of Suicide.org)

I do not want to make the theme of this book about suicide, but I will offer up my experience and the wisdom God gave me in a later chapter. I believe I went through one of the worst traumas imaginable, and nothing else this world could have offered could give me the perfect relief. Only Christ could have totally saved me. The primary theme of this book is all about Christ and the peace He has available for each and every one of us. The glory of my experiences belongs totally to Him. I want to emphasize again that no supposed inner strength in me could have ever kept me from going over the edge.

I had dreams in nights afterward where I was overlooking a huge cliff, like over the Grand Canyon. Suddenly I was falling a very long way to the bottom with increasing terror. I saw the rocks below on which I was about to splatter. Then suddenly that terror was completely erased as Christ reached out to catch me with His outstretched arms, cushioning my falling velocity. I am not one to remember most of my dreams afterward, but I do remember this one. It is a nightmare that turned out to be a very good dream. I have not had one of those dreams for many years now, and I realize that even in my sleep, God was reminding me of what had happened that day with its huge significance in the fact that Christ clearly rescued me that very morning from the very start, after my initial temptation to run away.

The Lord is my shepherd; I shall not want. He makes me
to lie down in green pastures; He leads me beside the still
waters. (Psalm 23:1–2)

A short while after my son's death, while the EMTs were taking out
the remains of my son, I was led to sit on the lawn outside our house
and meditate on the still waters and green pastures of Psalm 23:2. This
turned out to be the peace that Christ started right away in my mind, and
which developed more fully in me over hours, days, and years ahead. It
seemed immediate as I allowed myself to meditate on those words of that
oft-quoted Psalm, along with John 3:16. My mind was somewhat being
protected or guarded by simply reciting Bible verses. If I turned my mind to
the horror I'd just witnessed, all that peace left. That rest of the day turned
to be a giant lesson, where I probably spent six hours studying my Bible
late into the night; that peace seemed to be more lasting through God's
Word. Of course, that developed into a pure hunger for the Word. If I did
not allow my flesh to distract me from the horror I'd just witnessed, that
peace was (and now always is) there to go back to. I also remember praying
a lot that first day, as well as in the days to follow.

In the days, weeks, months, and years after my son's death, I guess I
wanted more assurances of where his soul or spirit went, and a couple of
questions kept plaguing me. "Where did my son go when he took his life?"
As I found myself being irresistibly drawn to Christ, this next question
followed the first one: "Did my son have to die for me to start to find Christ?"

And of course, I had much self-guilt over my son's suicide. A few
thousand what-ifs worked in my mind as to the many ways I could have
done things differently. I will write more in another chapter on Christ
guarding my heart and mind through His peace from Philippians 4:7, but
I will state here that I do believe Christ brought me to the right questions
and gave me the right assurances through His Word at the right times in
order to do that "guarding of my heart and mind."

The day after my son's death, I felt the need to go to a Catholic mass
early that morning, and later I went to my regular Church. Evidently the
Lord had a message for me in the Catholic church. During the homily of
that mass, the priest was speaking from Luke 23 on Christ's crucifixion.
That priest seemed to look directly at me and then quoted, "Father, forgive

them as they know not what they do" (verse 34). This turned out to be a message from God to me that provided a bit of trust that started that very day, to ease my mind from all my self-guilt and the thoughts I had over my son's salvation. It was not a complete understanding, but there was a bit of comfort.

Later, this verse below took on some solid meanings to me over the way I should trust God over my son's salvation.

> So, He said to them, "Assuredly, I say to you, there is no one who has left house or parents or brothers or wife or children, for the sake of the kingdom of God, who shall not receive many times more in this present time, and in the age to come eternal life." (Luke 18:29–30)

The verse became a bit clearer as I realize that my own journey in following Christ should not be inhibited by a lack of willingness to leave children, or in my case my son. In true application, I had to "leave" my wife who'd died eight years earlier. I needed to trust Christ even in my son's very salvation, along with my wife's salvation. It became a lesson that was I was to build upon for my children, even now.

Charles Stanley suggests this about suicide in his book *Handbook for Christian Living.*

> With this in mind, we can understand why there are so many questions concerning whether God forgives the person who commits suicide. After all, suicide is an act of rebellion against God. Fortunately for all of us, however, God's grace is without prejudice. Whoever believes will be saved. Nowhere in the Bible does God compartmentalize sin and reserve Grace for only those who commit "acceptable" sins. There is no such thing. Does God forgive suicide? Yes, He does.
>
> If the person who committed suicide at some accepted Jesus' death on the cross as payment for his sin debt and asked Him into his life, he is forgiven. Absolute assurance

of forgiveness is found in Romans 8:1 "There is therefore
no condemnation to those who are in Christ Jesus."

Now, twenty years later and though much Bible study and prayer, I
have never found anything to suggest I might be wrong in trusting Christ
on all that. In fact, I have now even more trust in Him over my son's
salvation. The answer to my many prayers that Christ put in my mind
initially has been this: "Since you now trust Me for your own salvation,
why would you not trust Me for your son's?"

In the end, we do serve an awesome GOD who can snatch victory
even from death. He did that very thing after all, though Christ on the
cross and then through His resurrection. I was a mere recipient of Christ's
perfect example.

4

More of This Peace

Then He arose and rebuked the wind, and said to the sea, "Peace,
be still!" And the wind ceased and there was a great calm.

—Mark 4:39

I've always liked this verse. Along with the few verses before and after it, I can envision Jesus standing up in the boat—maybe holding onto the mast for balance because the boat they were in was violently being rocked in the huge storm while it was being filled with water from the violent waves. The disciples were huddling together in fear, and maybe one or two of them desperately was bailing out the water coming into the boat with each wave. They were shouting out accusations to Christ because of His calmness in his sleeping. "Teacher, do you not care that we are perishing?" (Mark 4:38). A calmness from Christ seemed to indicate to them that He seemed to not care for their lives, because drowning seemed to be their ultimate fate.

Just then, Jesus suddenly wakes up, and with this same calmness and with total authority, he says, "Peace be still." Of course, the storm and the violent waves immediately calmed, and I can even see the disciples with wild-eyed amazement at what had just happened. Jesus then said to them, "Why are you so fearful? How is it that you have faith? And they feared exceedingly, and said to one another, 'Who can this be, that even the winds and the waves obey Him!'" (Mark 4:40-41)I think at that time, the disciples forgot about the storm they endured, and then they recognized that He was far more than a mere prophet—that He was God in the flesh who could control the elements of nature, just as He proved.

Scriptures do not tell us when in the night or early morning hours this particular event happened. I like to think it was just as the sun was just rising over the Galilean mountains on the new day. As they faced the violent storm for much of the nighttime hours with an increasing intensity, Christ rebuked that storm, the clouds parted, and they were suddenly bathed in the new day's early morning sunshine, along with the great calm in the waters of the Sea of Galilee. To me, it is a perfect picture of peace as only Christ can enact in our lives at any time.

This account in Mark, along with the same accounts in Matthew and Luke, signifies the great calming effect Christ can have on each us in our lives. As I faced the biggest storm in my life by seeing my only son in death and all the negative emotions that came with it, Christ said to my storm and said, "Peace be still."

Why am I so fearful at times? Why have I little or no faith at other times? This set of verses has been a lesson for me to remember vividly not only the storm that threatened me, but also where I was at one time in a situation where, but for the Grace of God, I was destined to drown in my own sorrows. It has become a promise and a fulfilling of that promise that I hold onto. Every time a new storm comes into my life, Christ says again, "Peace be still," to that storm. I can picture the clouds parting, the waves ceasing their violent actions, and a calming effect coming from Christ.

In the multi-church choir, I sang in, we sang one song that I loved, "Peace Be Still." I reflected on the words and the music of that song much in the days and months after my son's death. The song has a dramatic separation between the violence of the wind and waves of the storm, until the phrase "Peace be Still," where one can visually reflect on the stark difference with a musically enhanced calmness reflected by the words in the title of the song.

Music reflected in my mind has always been another source of peace, when I reflect on the words of Scripture in a Christian song. I suggest that for anyone as well. The hymns can add this sense of peace, especially when you are reflecting on the words of a hymn that directly quote Scripture or a promise in Scripture. It's even in a song that most of us learned as children: "Jesus loves me, this I know. For the Bible tells me so."

> And the peace of God, which surpasses all understanding, will guard your hearts and minds through Christ Jesus. (Philippians 4:7)

Over the years, I have found much more of the solid peace described in the verse. Coupled with this next verse, the word *peace* has become a bedrock of sorts to my growing faith that I can always find available in all discouragements and fears in my life. I have found that peace applicable in any and all situations, if I just look for it.

> Finally, brethren, whatever things are true, whatever things are noble, whatever things are just, whatever things are pure, whatever things are lovely, whatever things are of good report, if there is any virtue and if there is anything praiseworthy—meditate on these things. (Philippians 4:8)

This verse is telling us where to put our minds, or basically what we are to meditate on: whatever is true, noble, just, pure, lovely, of good report, with virtue, and praiseworthy. Meditating on only these things take a lot of practice, but it is certainly achievable in a growing faith in Christ.

Much is derived from the promise of the peace that Christ offers into our lives, the peace that He is ever ready to give to us when we turn to Him. For me, my former alcohol solution was to run away from God or hide from Him. My "solution" was of course worldly in nature and thus very imperfect—a false solution. Whether it be alcohol or drugs or really any other solution to try to pretend we can find peace, it is a worldly solution that is imperfect. The true peace can only come from Christ and is listed in this verse.

> Peace I leave with you, My peace I give to you; not as the world gives do I give to you. Let not your heart be troubled, neither let it be afraid. (John 14:27)

For nonbelievers, peace can be looked at as the promise that there is a solid assurance Christ is willing and able to change one's life from one of constant disappointments, lack of any hope, and a life filled with much fear over the future. You will learn, as I did, that the worldly solutions to finding that lasting peace in our lives is so incomplete and limited when compared to what even small faith in Christ can do to bring us to that lasting peace. We've started to see others who may have gone through a trauma in their lives, and then Christ rescued them, as he did for me. No magical prayer is needed, or being in the right church where the right prayers are said over you. Simply put, Christ is ready to come into the life of anyone, in any place, for those who truly humble themselves before Him at any time they cry out to Him. For me, all it took was three words: "Lord, help me," with a total humbleness before Him. He will reach people wherever they are at that moment in their lives, where the storms of life threaten to drown them.

For those of us who are believers in Him, peace adds to all this with the assurances derived from our salvation. We know the world we are living in is a temporary existence, and we have the peace knowing that a glorious new life awaits us someday. A lot of peace is derived from our lives where Christ has rescued us many, many times before. We have peace because He will do that rescuing again, no matter what comes our way. That God allows things to happen is our lives that might be problematic or even tragic will build us up to where our faith in Him is more complete.

I suggest here the importance of journaling. We should write down our highs and lows, our daily remembrances where we once have had our big and small problems. Then Christ's solution becomes evident. Then in the months and years afterward, we can look back and see from our own words how Christ rescued us.

In the years since my son's death, I have tried to determine what exactly happened when I was delivered from a deep, traumatic experience, as well as why I was delivered from it when others have gone over the edge and lost it afterwards. I read stories of soldiers suffering PTSD and look to psychobabble to explains things—all to better appreciate the huge miracle that Christ performed with me.

Christ saved me from falling off that proverbial cliff, and He soon delivered to me that growing peace that remains with me to this day. That same Christ is available to all of us, no matter what our experiences or hardships in life are.

Here is a very vivid example of what this peace looks like.

My son-in-law, Cory, is a captain on commercial airlines, and he generally flies different aircraft for each flight. He flies for a company that provides the flight crews for the shorter flights with the major airlines. He has related to me how, with all his pilot training, he has so much assurance and confidence in what he does as a career and with each aircraft he flies. He has spent many, many hours in the million-dollar flight simulators, plus many hours studying training manuals for each different model of plane he might be guiding through the air. All of this to train him beforehand to automatically respond to all emergencies that could conceivably come up in a flight on a particular aircraft he might be flying, such as an engine fire or a loss of rudder control. He relates that as he trains on these simulators, they also have programs for each of the different airports around the country, with their peculiar wind patterns for their take-off and landing conditions. Other factors to consider are the fact that before each flight, the captain and crew are notified of impending weather problems they might face in reaching their destination. They also examine maintenance logs for the individual aircraft they are flying, so that they know what to address if a problem comes up during the upcoming flight. As Cory relates it, that peace over his career leaves him on the way home in his commute from the airport, after he has landed.

In the few discussions with my Cory over his career, I have come to realize a definite form of this peace over what he does as a profession from all his training, and he passes on that peace to the passengers, usually through the cabin intercom system. This relative peace is simply from Cory's extensive training in all the potential what-if scenarios, plus knowing the aircraft he will be flying. I know that when I fly again, I will say something to the flight crew as a word of thanks for their professionalism and training after my flight has landed. I no longer take for granted this relative form of peace that I gain after a flight.

This relative peace is perhaps an incomplete form of the peace that I write about in my book, but it is a good example. But then, the peace I have discovered covers every aspect of our lives, and it is Christ who gives that perfect peace.

In a more complete application to this peace that we can derive from studying the Bible, we have a sixty-six-book training manual with a lot of simulations written into the history of God's dealings with mankind. The

Old Testament is filled with examples of men and women who turned to God, trusted God, and also strayed from God at times.

Right at the beginning, Adam and Eve had one command from God. Eve let Satan deceive her to question God, and Adam followed in her lead. Both partook of the forbidden fruit and were banished from the garden. They both tried to justify or explain away their own disobedience to God in Genesis 3:10–13. There's so much to learn from that very first simulated experience with the whole story in Genesis, chapters 2–3. Satan is willing to lead us away from God, using our pride to accomplish a distrust of God.

Noah trusted God to build an ark and save him and his family from the upcoming Judgment of God by flooding the whole earth. This is another example of a man who trusted God. Bible scholars tell us Noah's trust in God went on for 120 years as he and his sons built the ark to save them and their families from God's upcoming Judgment. I can imagine all the mocking he went through from others in those years as he was completing the ark. The "Lord saw the wickedness of man that was great upon the earth" (Genesis 6:5) and decided to destroy it, saving only Noah and his family, whose faith in God remained intact for all those years while they built the ark.

Abram (later renamed Abraham), who is also listed in Genesis and then as an example in the New Testament, is pointed out as a man who trusted God or had faith in God. God told him to leave his home in Haran, along with his family, and head to the land of Canaan, not knowing what they would find. His trust in God went on to the point where he was willing to sacrifice his own son, Isaac, in that trust in God, which he proved that he in fact trusted God. You can find His story throughout the Bible as a man who obeyed God and trusted in Him throughout his life.

Joseph, who went through many hardships, trusted God throughout his life and ended up second in command over all of Egypt. He saved many people, along with his extended family members, from the famine that came upon the world. He forgave his brothers for selling him into slavery at a young age, which he later concluded that "God sent me before you to preserve life" (Genesis 45:5). He saw God's hand in it all. Not only is his story about trusting God in good and bad situations, but it is a story about forgiveness and the deep need to forgive.

Moses became the leader of Israel, and God spoke through him with the laws God set down for the Israelites. Moses performed many miracles, where God displayed His glory and power through Moses prior to and during the exodus of the Israelites from Egypt.

King David is an example of a "man who was after God's own heart." He was anointed king over Israel by Samuel, the prophet, early on in his life. He showed his huge faith in God by defeating Goliath with a stone and his sling. The Bible tells us Goliath was well over nine feet tall, and yet David was not intimidated by size. He realized that God was infinitely more powerful, and he trusted God to overcome this giant of a man. David had to suffer much adversity and even ran for his life for fifteen years, before he was formally given the throne. He trusted God, and after many years when he was formally the king, he was eventually led by his own lust for Bathsheba to commit many sins. He was convicted by God through the prophet Nathan. He wrote many of the Psalms, and in Psalm 49 in particular, he laments over his sins by lusting after Bathsheba and ten ordering the death of her husband, Uriah. It's a clear example of restoration to God, and we can look to Christ now as the perfect restoration to God.

There were many more prophets in the Old Testament, where God spoke through them, and their words were written and recorded throughout history.

Then in the New Testament, we have Jesus Christ, who is God's way back to Him through His grace that He will afford to all of us. We can believe in or choose to reject Christ. The most oft-quoted verse makes it very plain as to our choice.

> For God so loved the world that He gave His only begotten
> Son, that whoever believes in Him should not perish but
> have everlasting life. (John 3:16)

The four Gospels have their unique and different narratives about the earthly life of God in the flesh, who emptied Himself to become as one of us. He healed the sick, opened the eyes of the blind, made the deaf hear, and even brought a few individuals back from death. Those examples are all significant because He was healing the sick, and we are all sick from our sins before we accept Christ. That He heals us through His grace and makes us well to stand before God.

> But He was wounded for our transgressions, He was bruised for our iniquities; The chastisement for our peace was upon Him, And by His stripes we are healed. (Isaiah 53:5)

We are truly blinded by the world we live in, before Christ opens our eyes and hearts to receive Him and desire to be healed.

> The Lord opens the eyes of the blind; The Lord raises those who are bowed down; The Lord loves the righteous. (Psalm 146:8)

We are "deaf" before we come to Christ and cannot receive His Word.

> In that day the deaf shall hear the words of the book, And the eyes of the blind shall see out of obscurity and out of darkness. (Isaiah 29:18)

And we are dead in our sins, before Christ gives us a new life.

> Even when we were dead in trespasses, made us alive together with Christ, by grace you have been saved. (Ephesians 2:5)

Even we Christians are guilty of not appreciating the blessings of a completed Bible—and we have an abundance of completed Bibles in whatever version we choose. We truly are those in which "much has been given," and the completed Bible in whatever form is available to us. I think we often take for granted our blessings on earth.

The Bible is our complete training manual with a lot of simulated situations from the many men and women who lived before us and found their own peace in following God. Through Jesus Christ, we have that perfect way to return to God. We have free will to believe in and accept Christ—or not. There is simply no other way.

Over the years since my son's death, I found another avenue in which I could maintain that peace and grow in my faith: Christian radio. There is a translator station here in remote Wyoming that I could listen to during the day and in the evenings after I got off work: Pilgrim Radio out of Carson City, Nevada. More recently we had another Christian radio station set up with a translator tower that is broadcast out of Havre, Montana. These avenues where I found Christian radio were to be a huge part of my life. The radio stations serve as another blessing that has gone on for twenty-two years, and they've helped me in growing my faith for all those years. We simply have no excuse when we cannot find Christ in this country.

As I drove a truck over the road for several years after my son took his life, another aid was the Bible on cassette tapes; the technology has gone from cassettes to CDs to iPods in the years since. I wore out some of those cassettes tapes in my hunger for the Word because I would even go to sleep in my truck while listening to them.

We are simply blessed with many ways through technology in which we can preserve our peace once we get it.

5

All Things Do Work Together

And we know that all things work together for good to those who
love God, to those who are the called according to His purpose.

—Romans 8:28

After my wife's death in 1987, I discovered something that aided me to
better be prepared in my son's death. It was something that helped me
with the question, "Where is God in all this?" It is in our human nature
to wonder if God took His eyes off our lives, or in this case my son's life.
Maybe God simply didn't care for a moment and let my son take his life;
maybe evil won out in that moment in time. As someone who was still not
a true believer in Christ before my son's death, I prayed for my son that very
morning and for a short while after his suicide. With my emotions, I said
to God, "This is the way you answer prayers, God? By allowing my son to
take his life?" Our emotions after a tragedy when a loved one is taken from
us will go in cycles. I wanted to hold onto my tiny belief and trust in Him
then, but I lashed out at God for a while when I took my eyes away from
this peace that was slowly developing in me though Christ's grace. God
has big shoulders, and as I have discovered, He allows and understands
our negative emotions for a time when we lash out at Him.

The day of my son's funeral, I do believe I was prepared to receive that
peace. I remembered a few things to look for after my wife's death eight
years earlier. As I struggled to see God in my situation, He showed up in

His creation—or in this case, the people who displayed their comfort and love in a variety of ways.

Before my son's funeral and shortly afterward, so many had come by our house with gifts of food and offers of places to stay for the family members who lived elsewhere and were coming for Larry's funeral. We received numerous sympathy cards from people who stopped by, and although they might not have known exactly what to say, they gave me and my daughter hugs in support. We even got anonymous gifts, where people did not want to identify themselves but wanted to give their support in some small way. I suppose this is a benefit of living in a small town, where the suicide of a young man brings out the love and concern for the family in many ways.

During Larry's funeral, I saw God in a two-year-old boy. My daughter and son had babysat for him a few months previously. "Geoff" grabbed a handful of Kleenex tissue and was moving from the laps of me and my extended family members in the first couple of rows of chairs, drying the eyes of each of us in turn. I believe most who attended were forced to smile over that gesture from a small child. God can show up in a small child in his innocence and concern, as was the case at my son's funeral with this young boy.

My sister and her husband, along with my parents, came over to my house the day after my son's death, wanting to clean up the "mess" in his room. That was a huge gesture because they felt this was our family's personal issue, and all four wanted to help in this very significant way. I know God moved them in this gesture, and even that day I was reminded there is a God, showing up in my extended family and in the young boy at the funeral. Their examples were a result of feelings led by God to give such loving gestures. I don't think I could have handled cleaning up the mess at the time, because I certainly did not want to face the evidence of what had transpired.

This is not to say that there were not negative reactions after my son's death. I found that there was a vicious rumor going around town that I had shot my own son. As the rumor went on, the police were about to charge me with murder, and they were waiting until after the funeral to formally charge me. I later discovered that this rumor was generated by some boys who had bullied my son in high school. Although they obviously felt their own regrets over his suicide, they were deflecting that guilt onto me. As a suggestion to anyone, let the good coming out of people overrule the bad reactions by others. It is inevitable because some people react negatively in their own guilt when such a thing as suicide happens.

After a loss, I recommend that anyone who has suffered a loss keep the cards as a remembrance for later to reflect upon. Gift notations in the attendance sign-in books that most funeral directors provide are aids so we can remember who to send thank-you cards to and reflect upon later. I am not ashamed as a man to admit that I cried a lot later when I brought out all the cards and the funeral book in the months and years after my son's funeral. I reflected on God's grace through His creation. I do believe tears are an aid in healing. In fact, I would like to reflect on a verse that is the shortest verse in the Bible in some translations.

Jesus wept. (John 11:35)

The context of this verse is in the account of the death of Lazarus, when Mary was in deep grief herself over her brother Lazarus's death. Now, even Christ, in knowing the miracle He was to soon perform in bringing Lazarus back to life, shared in Mary's grief at that moment. This is evidence of Christ who shares the grief of all of us in our moment of sorrow, even though He knows the bigger picture. My understanding of a Christ who sheds tears along with all of us in our sorrows is augmented in other verses as well. He is ever-ready to share in our sorrows, just as He did with Mary. We simply must recognize what He offers and thus believe in Him.

Christ does understand our individual weaknesses. From this verse, He shows He will be there with us through our trials, our temptations, and our own weaknesses.

> For we do not have a High Priest who cannot sympathize with our weaknesses, but was in all points tempted as we are, yet without sin. (Hebrews 4:15)

What an awesome thought. That Christ, as the high priest and in His love for us, is willing to help us face those temptations and trials we face. In 2015, around my own birthday (which was close to the twentieth anniversary of my son's death), I found something that was a wonderful reminder. My son took his life two days after my birthday in 1995, and stuck in with all those cards and that funeral book was a tiny, handmade card from Larry for my birthday in the year of his death. In it, he said to me through his teenaged humor, "You are a good father." It seems that that little card was forgotten about and then not seen or discovered until twenty years later. The tears came back to me when I found that card. I do believe God continues to bless us in our losses—and in my case, twenty years after that loss.

6

Peace through God's Restoration

And the LORD restored Job's losses[a] when he prayed for his friends.
Indeed the LORD gave Job twice as much as he had before.

—Job 42:10

One unexpected aspect in learning to mostly trust God is in what God prepared for me later, after I lost a wife and then a son. I was to eventually marry a widow who is fourteen years younger than me, and I took on three new children. The youngest boy, Casey, was four at the time.

Certainly, God had prepared me beforehand a bit more in my losing my loneliness. I can remember the exact moment where I felt the huge presence of Christ in my life, and that need for a woman in my life, derived from loneliness, was never to be a factor again. I was content in my situation as a single man who was seeking out Christ, which was exactly the lesson God had provided for me in my life at the right time.

Two years after that experience, I was to meet Marti in the church we both attended. We have now been members of that church for sixteen years. In marrying her, I had many concerns and fears. I was fifty-one at the time, and taking on three new children was certainly not a goal I would ever have thought was in my future. This was coupled with the fact that Marti was many years younger. I'd lost a son to suicide, and so I had not imagined God giving me more children to care for. But as it turned out, God had prepared me beforehand to take on the role of husband and father to these children. It was an unexpected, new direction that God provided me in desiring to marry Marti. God, in his directions for my life, entrusted me to be a father to even more children. He provided to me a lot of convincing through a lot of prayers that this was indeed what He had planned for my life for the future. Remembering back to that convincing of God that this was indeed His direction He had planned for my life has served me well in the last fifteen years of our marriage. I never had a doubt that I had made a mistake. If we put Christ at the center of our marriage, all would go well.

"Out of the mouth of a child" innocence was certainly in Casey when, at four years of age a couple of months before I asked his mother for her hand in marriage, he said, "You going to be my new dad?" It was as if he was already convinced of it all and sensed my reluctance. That young boy turned out to be a very responsible young man who is now in his second year of college. I am truly proud to be Casey's dad.

Like Job, with God restoring to him so much, I was to receive another of these blessings of restoration: my wife and I had Jasper together a year after we married. I had three new sons, and God added a new daughter to boot! It is all very significant regarding the fact that I felt guilt over not being there for Larry before his suicide, coupled with the fact that I'd failed as a father. But God would eventually entrust me with four new children. When one learns to trust God, one should not be surprised. I essentially gave my son up to God, and He eventually restored to me four new children to love and care for. I believe He blesses us with a restoration of sorts later in life, and He does restore to us in a variety of ways when we learn to trust Him, even in our losses.

It's so wonderful that when God selects our mates, He also gives us the assurances that Christ will never leave or forsake us in or marriage. That promise has been in me for fifteen years now, and our marriage is far more solid that it was when we first married. Marti and I have taught marriage classes in our church as a couple whose perspective came from two individuals who had failed a lot in our previous marriages. We now have discovered Christ's way, putting Him in the center of our marriage. We can relate to the many problems that come up in many other marriages, having gone through similar problems ourselves.

When we were getting the license for our marriage in 2002, the clerk at the courthouse had to ask us, "What number is this marriage for each of you?" That number goes on the license. Both of us admitted that it was the fifth for both of us, and I remember the look on that clerk's face, as if to say, "You two setting records here?"

Certainly, Marti and I have had our ups and downs in the fifteen years of our marriage. But we try to keep Christ at the center of our marriage, and He continues to bless this union. Two can become one, as we've both been reminded of at a couple of Weekend to Remember Christian Marriage retreats that we attended a few years ago, This program from Family Life has strengthened our marriage. I and Marti have been so blessed because we are endeavoring to more fully understand the aspect of two becoming one in a Christ-centered marriage. That aspect is certainly described with this verse.

> Therefore a man shall leave his father and mother and be joined to his wife, and they shall become one flesh. (Genesis 2:24)

As I look back at my very rich and blessed life for the past fifteen years since I married Marti and became the father of four new children, I cannot help but think God has blessed me in abundance. The following verse comes to mind as well.

> So He said to them, "Assuredly, I say to you, there is no one who has left house or parents or brothers or wife or children, for the sake of the kingdom of God, ³⁰ who shall not receive many times more in this present time, and in the age to come eternal life," (Luke 18:29–30)

In my trust in God, I had to leave my deceased wife and son in His hands. Through those losses, I learned to trust Him even more through the wonderful Grace Christ has been affording me all those years since those losses. "Not my will, but Thine be done" (Luke 22:42).

When we become closer to Christ and learn to trust in Him, He does share with us through the Holy Spirit some of the ways He prepared us before we came to Him, and He continues to prepare us through our lives for new avenues where we serve Him in many ways. Maybe it's a glimpse of the bigger picture as God sees it. Regarding each piece in the puzzle in our lives from the past, by looking at them in any moment in time, we can see a better picture of how God has been preparing us. We realize how we gained good through our many trials in the past, and even from His new directions at times, where we wondered about being felt led to do something that we couldn't have guessed to do on our own.

7

Peace in Life versus Death

For to be carnally minded is death, but to be
spiritually minded is life and peace.

—Romans 8:6

I had an experience in January 2016 where I was face with my own immortality and found the blessed peace regarding whether or not I was to succumb to possible cancer.

I had what was originally diagnosed as a stomach flu that wasn't getting better after a few days. I eventually went to an urgent care, a walk-in clinic that is also open on weekends. There, they initially confirmed the stomach flu diagnosis but did blood tests on me and sent me to get prescriptions for this supposed flu. While waiting at the pharmacy to have my prescriptions filled, I got a call from this clinic and was told that I needed to get to the ER immediately. From their blood tests, it indicated that I had a severe case of pancreatitis.

After relating that message to my wife, Marti, she told me that was exactly what her deceased husband was diagnosed with before he eventually succumbed to cancer in 1999. Our anxiety heightened. We uttered a quick prayer together as she rushed me to the ER of the hospital.

The doctors there had a bit of problem coming up with a firm diagnosis. I had had an operation in my lower abdomen forty years before, which was somewhat masking the problems. But even then, Christ was guarding my heart and mind, as well as Marti's (Philippians 4:7), due to our simple prayer. The surgeon was called in and ordered an emergency operation for me the next morning, telling me he did not know what he would find other than my gall bladder, which looked as if it needed to be removed. Cancer was a big possibility. I do not remember one anxious moment where I was particularly concerned over what the doctors would find.

While lying on the gurney before I was taken in for surgery early that next morning, I had the peace of God flooding me. I knew I did not have any big regrets in life, and certainly my wife and children would be taken care of. The song "His Eye Is on the Sparrow, and I Know He Watches Me" continually played in my mind. That song comes from this verse.

> But the very hairs of your head are all numbered. Do not fear therefore; you are of more value than many sparrows. (Luke 12:7)

When I woke up from surgery later that morning, the first person I saw was the surgeon, who told me, "Jim, it was just your gall bladder, which we removed. No cancer of any form." My wife soon learned of the news, and we gave our praises to God that He had spared me.

I feel my peace from God has essentially been completed in a sense, because through the issue of my own life-or-death wonderment, I found it even then. Now I want to present that peace to all who lack it in their own lives. From Philippians 4:7, "Christ will guard our hearts and minds through this Peace" if we firmly place our trust in Him. Through our humble "prayers and petitions," He will grant us that peace because we know He is watching over us when we truly believe in and trust Him.

> You will keep in perfect peace all who trust in you, all whose thoughts are fixed on you! (Isaiah 28:3 NLT)

That perfect peace is such a blessing, where you can fully trust God even in life versus death. If He decides we are to leave this earth, I am ready.

8

Peace over Our Children

Evil people will surely be punished, but the
children of the godly will go free.

—Proverbs 11:21 (NLT)

Marti and I have six children combined. Five are out on their own, and we have Jasper still at home as a seventh grader. Of course, I lost another son as well.

There have been lots of ups and downs with them, but I believe the Lord has given me a peace over them and the choices they make in their lives, coupled with the fact that all have been grounded in Christ Jesus. I always must go back to the lesson I learned with my deceased son, which is turning them over to God and trusting in Him.

My daughter Dawn, who lost her brother in 1995 and her mother in 1978, has been an example to me of how I, as a father, can better be there for her even after she left home after graduating from high school. I trust in God for her future. She will admit she ran from God for many years after she lost her brother, and for a while, I believe she blamed me a bit for his death, along with her blaming God. She also admitted she didn't have any good memories of her deceased mother. As my faith in Christ grew, I wrote many letters over the years to her about this peace I felt through Christ, along with memories of her mother that I had. I helped her recognize that her mother was a very special person, but just as immature as I was back then. I made many prayers over my daughter Dawn over all these years, and I believe God protected her in her running from Him. He eventually brought her back to Christ about two years ago. This was significant because her goal was always to get married and start a family. We both agree she was finally ready because she was at the point in her life where all the anger and bitterness had been removed by Christ. Her renewed faith in Christ was growing. In August 2015, after she finally met the man God had prepared for her, she went on to marry him. I had the honor to give her away as a father in their wedding ceremony in Colorado.

I turned my daughter over to God, as well as my son who took his life, and I believe that aspect can work for all parents of children who are adults and on their own. My added aspect there with Dawn was to always think of her, call occasionally, and write many letters.

Maybe I am old-fashioned, but I do believe a hand-written letter is far more personal. When we write to encourage, using Bible verses as I did for all those years, I believe it encourages the recipient (and us) when we write about Jesus Christ. In this technology-savvy world, the aspect of sitting down and writing a letter is the best form of communication, and I recommend it to anyone. It has been a blessing for my life, and as I have found, the Word never comes back to us void. That is, I do believe when we share God's Word, it tends to encourage us as well in our sharing. Over the last twenty years, my list of people I write to regularity has grown, including writing letters to two prisoners.

Right now, our two younger adult children have somewhat left the Christian faith. Our youngest daughter is studying anthropology and has adopted a lot of evolutionary theories. She and I have had a few debates over all that, but I still maintain a peace that God has it all in control. Her mother and I must turn her over to Him because it will not be us who brings her back to the Christian faith, but God. There must be an *if* in all that. We should not put up walls against her due to our disagreements about Christ. We must simply point out to her how proud we are of her achievements over the last four years in her college education, and how well she has done in all that. We are keeping those lines of communication open, and I write letters to her about Christ without preaching, as well as her mother talking to her a lot on the phone.

This wonderful young lady called me up the day after my surgery in January 2016 and told me how much she appreciated me as a father for the last fifteen years of her life. I believe her mother related how potentially serious my operation was. These moments, when we feel really blessed, are memories to cherish always. I am truly rich beyond measure as to her appreciating me as a father who took over after the death of her biological father, and I have never had any regrets in adopting three new children in my marriage to Marti. I also got a call that day from the older son with much the same appreciation, me and I will never forget what was said by both.

We all must give our adult children up to God and keep the communication aspect very open, as Christ-believing parents. We must learn to accept, but not always endorse, their choices in their lives, if they have left what they were grounded with in their Christian faith. Our two younger adult children are going through their individual belief-system differences right now, but with my trust in God, I must always go back to the fact that I have turned them over to Him. Our son Casey, who is now in his first semester in college, and I have had many father-son conversions that invariably end up discussing matters of faith. I see him now as someone who has explored the different belief systems (including atheism), and God could make him a great apologist for the Christian faith. But I must trust in God on all that.

I believe we worry about our adult children, and sometimes needlessly. We should always pray for them, but we must trust God on their journeys in life. I know for me, like all my children before, they have made the decision at one time to accept Christ in their lives. Although we wish that they would live their lives in accordance to their faith, it doesn't always work out that way.

This part of peace over our children who have reached adulthood is essential.

9

Peace through a Resistance to the Conformity of the World

And do not be conformed to this world, but be transformed
by the renewing of you mind, that you may prove what is
that good and acceptable and perfect will of God.

—Romans 12:2

One aspect I've discovered to help me preserve God's peace is in the areas where I allow in myself these little conformities to the world that divert my attention from this peace. The world around us in American society, which I of course live in, has a lot of "me first" people in it and a lot of "buy more, do more, see more, experience more, and be more" attitudes that infect all of us as believers, whether a little or a lot. Marketing is clearly aimed toward the lusts we can been deceived by, for all the things we think we must have to supposedly make our lives richer and supposedly fuller. This goes along with the peace we think we can gain by having more worldly possessions, versus the real peace through Christ. As my wife and I are discovering, we need to have solid distinction between what would be considered necessity versus luxury. The world's marketing powers are very much around us.

A good example of the powers of marketing was when Larry and my daughter Dawn were growing up around the time McDonald's restaurants were becoming a huge force in America. Their barrage of television ads then were filling our children's minds with pictures of the golden arches, and Ronald McDonald the clown was making appearances in their restaurants. I do believe my daughter Dawn could say "donalds" and pick out the golden arches from two blocks away while we were driving, before she could say "Mommy" or "Daddy." We set our children before the television for much of the day, with its countless commercials on all the cartoon programming.

That same example of the marketing forces is very problematic in us adults as well, and over the years I have done my fair share of impulse buying—a lot from just walking into a home improvement store, for example. Now as a new creation in Christ, I have realized that this subtle conformity generated by the world around us is very powerful in its deceiving. When Marti and I married, cancelling our cable television programming was one of the first things we did because our two youngest children were mesmerized by watching it all, along with the constant barrage of commercials aimed toward their childlike greed to plead for new toys and games. Now, we have computer streaming, but we can control it a bit better for our thirteen-year-old son.

Coupled with the fact that the content of television programming has gone so far downward (where what would be a PG-13 rating now would be considered an R rating thirty years ago) is the fact that we have let the huge force of commercialization come into our homes. Our television viewing habits can be a double-edged sword. We should be concerned about the content of the television programs we or our children watch, but we should also be concerned by the commercials that tempt us with our lusts to buy more, do more, and have more. It simply became more evident in my older children thirty years ago that we can be adapt a conformity to the world, which in turn robs us of our peace through Christ, or at least take our eyes off the perfect peace.

In this computer age, where we have pop-up ads to get us to buy more stuff, it is an increasing challenge to resist that temptation to accumulate more possessions and supposedly enrich our lives by more buying. I believe the conditions of the perilous times of the Last Days, as described in Paul's second letter to Timothy, are all around us in abundance.

> But know this, that in the last days perilous times will
> come: For men will be lovers of themselves, lovers of money,
> boasters, proud, blasphemers, disobedient to parents,
> unthankful, unholy, unloving, unforgiving, slanderers,
> without self-control, brutal, despisers of good, traitors,
> headstrong, haughty, lovers of pleasure rather than lovers
> of God, having a form of godliness but denying its power.
> And from such people turn away! (2 Timothy 3:1–5)

We can see countless examples of each of these "conditions of men" around us in such abundance, and we can develop a relative conformity to these conditions as believers.

10

Peace through Forgiveness

But if you do not forgive, neither will your Father
in heaven forgive your trespasses.

—Mark 11:26

This verse points to the part of the Lord's Prayer where we say we forgive others for their trespasses as we are forgiven by God. It's a two-part thing because to be forgiven, we must forgive others. And in application, we carry burdens in our lives until we have forgiven others for the many things we have experienced in our past.

My two-week stay in the counseling center in California a few months before my son took his life was to be a seed of learning the aspect of forgiveness that God gave me, and it increased for many years afterward.

I do believe my earthly father and his frustration over me as a young boy was the primary root of my need for forgiveness of others. As I learned to forgive my father, other things from my past and who did what to me were far easier to gain regarding this forgiveness. A true humbleness before God makes us realize that we should hope others we have wronged will forgive us as well, especially in my being a selfish, rebelling jerk for so many years before I came to Christ.

As I mentioned earlier, I was not cut out to take over my father's ranch, yet my dad certainly wanted it to be that way because I was the only boy. I discovered that I had one repressed memory of my father beating me unmercifully in front of my friends and other adults when I was thirteen or fourteen. This was the start of my solid rebellion against him, which went on for some thirty years. By humbly knowing my own frustration and realizing how I handled it all as an adult myself, I was essentially copying my father's frustration and anger for many years. Humbly realizing I needed forgiveness for myself over my many displays of anger and frustration toward my children and my deceased wife when I became an adult made it easy for me to find forgiveness for my dad. We do copy our parents' good and bad examples, whether we do in fact realize. That fact or not.

In this counseling center, they used an example in a group setting where fifteen of us sat around in a circle. We were instructed to pass around a Styrofoam cup, where we each tore out a page of a big LA phone book, wadded it up, and stuffed it inside the cup. As you can guess, the cup ended up bursting down the sides after the tenth person shoved in a wadded-up page. This is precisely what goes on with us when we have all this unforgiveness toward others. We end up having this junk inside us, and nothing is ever resolved or let free by Christ. We burst out in our anger and frustration because of all this junk inside us, and we cannot handle one more piece of junk. I knew that many in that counseling center at the time I was there had far worse situations in their lives, with some who had been sexually abused as children. The aspect is still the same.

That is a concept in learning how to forgive. You notice that people have gone through worse situations in their lives. Our pain for our pasts almost seems insignificant compared to, for instance, a woman who had been sexually abused as a child, or an a young man who had witnessed his mother's murder as a child.

Corrie Ten Boom, in her book *The Hiding Place*, uses as one of her examples that awesome power of forgiveness from and through Christ. After her message on forgiveness in a church service, she was confronted by a former German SS guard who was one of her jailers during World War II. As she relates, "As I took his hand the most incredible thing happened. From my shoulder along my arm, a current seemed to pass from me to him, while into my heart sprang a love for this stranger that almost overwhelmed me." She knew she needed to truly forgive that man for the horrors she went through many years earlier, and she gave a simple prayer:

"Lord Jesus, forgive me and help me to forgive him." At that point, she and the former SS guard were equal; they both needed Christ's forgiveness.

What an awesome power Christ offers us in simply forgiving others who have wronged us. Only Christ can grant us that ability to forgive and thus set us free and give us a vital aspect of the peace from His removing all that junk that is inside us.

As to my dad, I was rewarded with a closeness to him that I never had before for the last eight or nine years before he passed on. I totally forgave him for my childhood experiences. In fact, I was to hold his hand in his last few hours and give him the assurance that I would take care of Mom, before he succumbed to the cancer raging though his body. Along with my oldest daughter, Amber, I told him about the True Christ through reading many Scripture verses and through a lot prayersover him. A few months before that, I felt led to write him a long letter on all the good aspects he gave me while I was growing up. We had many good, long talks in those final years, and I found the forgiveness towards him through Christ. We enjoyed our new father-son relationship before he passed on in 2005.

The other huge aspect for me regarding forgiveness was toward the other woman who was with my wife the night she died. I admit here that my opinions (derived from my questions over the accident) resulted in my blame. Certainly, forgiveness for myself was a huge factor over aborting what would have been our third child with Darlene in 1977. It is amazing, the grace Christ has afforded, not only did He forgive me, but He let me find forgiveness for myself over it all. God entrusted me with new children to raise in His new direction for my life.

I found more of this blessed peace from Christ by forgiving this woman, my father, and myself, as well as everyone in my past who hurt me in some way. I do believe I carried around a burden on my back for much of my life. Christ promises us freedom here, and freedom is a solid release from our lack-of-forgiveness burdens.

> Stand fast therefore in the liberty by which Christ has made us free,[1] and do not be entangled again with a yoke of bondage. (Galatians 5:1)

    This verse refers to the bondage of sin we carry around before we come to Christ, but it also refers to the freedom He affords us when we find forgiveness for others who have hurt or wronged us—and for ourselves. As Mark 11:26 tells us, we must forgive in order to be forgiven and thus enjoy this freedom. Christ will make us completely free if we turn over all our cares and woes over to Him. He is the great healer.

11

Peace Despite Politics

Beware lest anyone cheat you through philosophy and empty
deceit, according to the tradition of men, according to the
basic principles of the world, and not according to Christ.

—Colossians 2:8

The 2016 election results have been decided, and we have a new president.
I must once again go back to this verse in Colossians, which tells me
what transpired in this election, like most before it. We are letting the
"philosophy and empty deceit, according to the traditions of men,"
through all the campaign rhetoric, make our decisions for us. It really
didn't matter who won or lost in this election. This nation is divided by
a lot false rhetoric that generally makes one side look good and the other
side evil. It's generated by the two major political parties and their pundits.
Fear certainly is being transmitted as well—fear over Muslims, fear over
immigrants, fear over the new president getting us into unwanted wars.

It is telling that according to news sources, the Russians had some
influence on this election. They used social media to influence this election,
just like they possibly did in previous elections.

"Not according to Christ" in that Colossians verse means we are
letting all this empty deceit of men guide our lives instead of Christ. Some
even make idols out of their politicians, as if they are saviors, instead of
Christ as the only Savior.

And of course, the driving force in politics is all the special interest groups and their huge infusions of money to finance the candidates who will best serve their interests. Segments of the population are being guided by these issue ads that best serve their own individual needs and pretend to eliminate the fears we can sometimes adopt. We are at the brink of collapse in this country because so little that has come out in the campaigns in the last year can be construed as truth, or at really truth that has no attached bias.

I do believe God is turning us over as a nation to our own devices. As the adage goes, "We don't elect the politicians that we think we want, but the politicians that we deserve." We might be in for a very bumpy ride in the next few years because things could get conceivably worse.

As Christians, we try to falsely combine our Christian ideals and the worldly nature of politics, as if voting for or against a candidate might be how we think God would want us to vote. Many simply adapt the false rhetoric coming out of the campaigns and the political pundits, as if they all were speaking from God. Like the nonbelievers, we adopt the fears garnered by one side or the other, and even disdain or even adopt hatred toward candidates on the opposing side.

The political divide in this country has become so bad that I read a news article a while ago stating two Christians were screaming at each other because each was going to vote for different presidential candidates, and they were each mad at the other for their foolish choices. When did worldly politics become a source of major doctrines or beliefs? Have we, in the Body of Christ, conformed to the world so much that we are ready to brand others as heretics simply because they view the "lesser of two evils" differently?

The election has now been decided, and things may calm down a bit. Hopefully the protests will die down. But that worldly divide will remain under the surface until God grants this nation, or the Christian believers in this nation, an awakening. As a whole, we have lost any semblance to the salt and light of Christ in this very troubled world. This is not to say there are not a lot of solid believing Christians in this nation, but collectively we do not represent what we proclaim.

I am not any sort of eschatologist, but I do believe some of the signs of the Last Days are here now, as they have been for two thousand years since Christ walked the earth. Just before the rise of the antichrist or the conditions of the "Force of the anti-Christ" come forward, we are not suddenly going to find ourselves in brand-new conditions, such as those listed in the many prophesies of the Last Days. Those conditions will always be present and at times will intensify. I do believe they are certainly more in evidence right now.

When asked about the signs of the Last Days by His apostles in the Olivet Discourse in Matthew 24, Christ starts out very significantly in verse 4 by saying, "Take heed that no one deceives you." That's a very clear warning that deception will be tantamount now, just as it has been a force throughout the history of the Bible. His warning at the first of this discourse is a major warning of something to resist as things get worse. We Christians are allowing and even adopting into our own lives a lot of worldly deception through the political forces derived from the moneyed interests to get us to vote one way or another. Lots of false prophets tell us to be very fearful if the opposing candidate is elected, and they state what their candidate will do to turn around this nation. As listed in Matthew 24:11, they will "deceive many."

> *The coming of the lawless one is according to the working of Satan, with all power, signs, and lying wonders, and with all unrighteous deception among those who perish, because they did not receive the love of the truth, that they might be saved. And for this reason, God will send them strong delusion, that they should believe the lie.* (2 Thessalonians 2:9–11)

I believe when we pay more attention to politics and go to our one-sided sources for "truth," it tends to unsettle us. We are really looking for relative truths. In periods in my life where I paid more attention to politics and not to "whatever things are of good report" (Philippians 4:8), I tend to get more agitated. We simply must gain a love or truth in all forms and rely less on our worldly opinions, which are often misguided.

I picked up a copy of *Time Magazine* recently, which I do not normally read. On the cover it said, "Is Truth Dead?" It got me to thinking that even the editors of a secular magazine are sensing there is something wrong, particularly in a political fashion, where truth is only relative.

> Finally, brethren, whatever things are true, whatever
> things are noble, whatever things are just, whatever things
> are pure, whatever things are lovely, whatever things are of
> good report, if there is any virtue and if there is anything
> praiseworthy—meditate on these things. (Philippians 4:8)

What we have is a condition where the world has set up its many deceptions via our political discourses, and many political commentators have not the love of truth, or all truth, in giving their commentaries. As a Christian believer, you have to separate what is of God and what is of the world via our political discourses; make those lines of separation distinct. There is an underlying indoctrination (via the world) going on, centered around politics where people on both side of the political divide are espousing their truths—and not necessarily God's truth.

In this world around us, I ponder on these verses, as well as the teachers we sometimes set up to tell us what we want to hear in a political fashion.

> For the time will come when they will not endure sound
> doctrine, but according to their own desires, because
> they have itching ears, they will heap up for themselves
> teachers; and they will turn their ears away from the truth,
> and be turned aside to fables. (2 Timothy 4:3–4)

No, these very biased political commentators are not teaching doctrine per se, but they are leading people astray in their application of sound doctrine. Sometimes people collectively hear what they want to hear, and truth is based on what people want to believe according to their political biases.

We simply must remember God is in control, and in the last few elections that fact is more evident. "Not according to Christ" is the way I must look at the political atmosphere in this country. I really must follow the directives of this verse regarding how I look at politics and the clear and obvious deceptions in worldly politics.

> And He said to them, "Render therefore to Caesar the
> things that are Caesar's, and to God the things that are
> God's." (Luke 20:25)

When asked about paying taxes, Jesus replied that Caesar represented the world we live in, as to a deeper understanding of what He really said. That is far different than the God we worship. Our allegiance to Caesar (in the form of politicians and the political parties they represent) should be far different than the "things that are God's."

I believe that for the peace I try to maintain, I try to look to independent sources for my news. One wants to stay somewhat informed, but one must recognize that in this world, there is so much that is biased in our news. One will get unsettled or even angry when one follows the bias (and believes in it) from the political debates and forgets that God ultimately is in control.

The other thing to remember is that our opinions are oftentimes what we want to believe, and thus they are very relative.

12

Suicide (or the Lack of Hope as the Cause)

For we are aliens and pilgrims before You, As were all our fathers; Our days on earth are as a shadow, And without hope.

—1 Chronicles 29:3

In the past few years, I have tried to determine why my son took his life. Why did he do what he did? What was the common element that led to his suicide? What element contributed to his lack of hope in the final moments in his life, and what pushed him over the edge?

Two aspects I have determined is that Larry really did not want to exist without his mother. Her impact on his life was huge, and he didn't want to go on with life without her. I saw a lot of signs, shortly after his funeral from his secular counselor and others who knew him, that indicated there was a side to him that wasn't so readily seen. Certainly, the aspects of his being bullied in school contributed to it, and these two elements pushed him over the edge with increasing intensity. A good analysis is this one.

> A major cause of suicide is the despair of living without meaning or purpose. In a world overwhelmed with violence, divorce, homelessness, disease, and drug abuse, it is often the norm to live life bouncing around without anything to hold onto that would give meaning or security to an otherwise lonely existence.

The fact that many children are finding suicide to be logical choice underscores the impact that the pressures of life, even at an early age, can have. They live a world of isolation, rejection and the perception that no one cares. Life becomes intolerable, and suicide is the "logical" answer. Depression is the key factor in most suicides. *(Charles Stanley's Handbook for Christians Living)*

There clearly is no visible hope without Christ for many of our nation's youths, and for adults as well. I often think about what an impact we Christians could have if each of us were to mentor one child not in our immediate families. This lack of hopelessness in our nation would be significantly reduced by Christians reaching out and sharing their faith. Planting seeds particularly in our youth in this country would provide them with an alternative to this lack of hope. We are trying to come up with all these government "solutions" to curb the suicide rates, but we each should try to take care of our tiny corners of the world.

The ideal is that we must be "salt and light" to the unbelieving world—a world filled with violence, hopelessness, and despair. We who have found the trust and hope in our salvation in God are not doing a very good job of reaching out to those who are filled with a lack of hope.

And are confident that you yourself are a guide to the blind, a light to those who are in darkness. (Romans 2:19)

This applies to not only the youth that have a sense of hopelessness but also to all who we meet in a chance encounter. The light we have in Christ needs to be shared in a world filled with so much hopelessness.

The number of Christians in America has held steadily at 73 percent, according to Barna Research. With such a clear majority of people who profess a faith in Jesus Christ, why is there such a clear lack of hope? I think the above article from *Charles Stanley's Handbook on Christian Living* can be summed up as a lack of solid hope that comes through Jesus Christ and is depicted in this verse.

> Now hope does not disappoint, because the love of God
> has been poured out in our hearts by the Holy Spirit who
> was given to us. (Romans 5:5)

My thoughts are that we, as believers in Christ, should be sharing so much more of this hope to a world filled with such despair and with a clear lace of hope. We believers in Christ have the awesome power to deliver hope to others through the light of Christ, which we have been given. I pray for an awakening in this country, as well as in other countries around the world, that there really is an answer to that lack of hope in so many, which is Jesus Christ and the peace He can give us when we trust in Him.

13

Peace of God versus
Peace with God

"There is no peace," says the LORD, "for the wicked."

—Isaiah 48:22

One aspect of coming to a true faith in Christ is realizing that we are the "wicked" in this verse. We need a Savior because "all have sinned and fall short of the glory of God" (Romans 3:23). That is why God offers us His only begotten Son as a Savior to achieve the "everlasting life" in the following verse.

> For God so loved the world that He gave His only begotten
> Son, that whoever believes in Him should not perish but
> have everlasting life. (John 3:16)

In God's love for us, He offered up Christ to pay the penalty for our sins. You simply cannot have the peace of God unless you address some questions: "Have I made peace with God? Have I accepted that Jesus is my Savior, and do I truly believe in Him? Have I addressed the fact that, as a sinner, I need a Savior?"

We must truly humble ourselves before God, just as I did when I said the simple prayer of "Lord, help me" on the day my son took his life. I was truly at a place in my life where the alternative solution didn't look good, and I was tired from running. His grace effectively caught me from running away, and it truly humbled me.

> But he giveth more grace. Wherefore he saith, God resisteth the proud, but giveth grace unto the humble. (James 4:6)

This theme of "humbleness before Him" is all throughout the Bible, word for word: James 4:6, Psalm 138:6, Proverbs 3:34, and 1 Peter 5:5.

That aspect was the turning point in my life, where I offered up the simple prayer of "Lord, help me." I was drawn toward these feeling of calmness, and I discovered more by simply reading His Word. I saw myself as a sinner in a desperate need of a Savior. I effectively needed the gospel of Christ in my life.

The gospel of Christ can be summed up in four very vital steps.

1] Who are we accountable to? God.
2] What is our problem? Sin (through Adam) that separates us from God.
3] What is God's perfect solution to our problem? Jesus Christ.
4] What is my decision? To realize a faith in Christ, and to turn to Him.

The first step in the process is the hardest to realize. Unless we humble ourselves before God and realize the absolute need for God's perfect solution, we cannot believe in the completed gospel of Christ.

I truly believe that finding faith in the completed gospel of Christ, which is essentially summed up here, can lead us to this verse.

> And the peace of God, which surpasses all understanding, will guard your hearts and minds through Christ Jesus. (Philippians 4:7)

The peace of God is firmly established through our trust in Him and though His promises to us.

14

Peace in Our Health

You will keep him in perfect peace, Whose mind
is stayed on You, because he trusts in You.

—Isaiah 26:3

Midway through writing this book, I suffered a minor stroke. It was not a major one in which one side of my body would have been affected, and although my balance was problematic for a short time afterward, that soon went away. An MRI showed a bit of brain damage, and I had to learn again how to comprehend by essentially rerouting my thought process. Because of that brain damage, for about two months I lost any sort of confidence that I could finish this book or have a normal comprehension. But then I remembered thinking one day, "Why not apply this trust in God that I have to help me learn how to put my thoughts together?" As I prayed for God to help me in this endeavor to essentially reroute my brain, that peace flooded me as it had in so many other situations in my life. I had a problem also with my speech patterns. I could not put thoughts together in a rational pattern, so I stayed silent in conversations with my wife in particular. But as it turned out for me, the brain is a marvelous thing because it can reroute itself despite the dead areas that come from a stroke.

Our pastor's grandson was born with a condition called cerebellar hypoplasia, which is a condition from an underdeveloped brain in the womb. When it was first discovered, "Josiah" would likely not be able walk or function as a normal boy, according to the medical specialists. Today, some ten years later, he not only can walk and run, but he has mastered the art of learning. He is now a sixth grader in our school system. Of course, his family never told him he was disabled but encouraged him through his trials. His example has been a great inspiration for me.

My niece, Teri, has been another inspiration to me. She has been in a wheelchair for over twenty years. Her spinal cord in her back was compressed due to a falling accident. She has never walked in all that time and suffers a lot of pain. She even drives her own van with hand controls to and from work and church. She has remained a Christian all these years, and despite the severe pain that comes with her condition, she trusts in the Lord. Recently she has received an experimental drug that is supposed to relieve the pain without having to rely on heavy narcotics, and we are all praying that the drug will do what it is supposed to do.

My neighbor's son, Bruce, who has had spinal bifida since birth and has never walked in his life, has been another inspiration for me. He is now in his late forties and gets around town in his wheelchair. Nothing seems to trouble him.

We can all find situations where people are suffering a lot worse that we are. Christ opens our eyes and show us that others are enduring while keeping their faith in Christ.

15

Trusting in the Sovereignty of God

Trust in the LORD with all your heart, and lean
not on your own understanding;
In all your ways acknowledge Him, And He shall direct your paths.

—Proverbs 3:5–6

At some point in a true believer's life, one must acknowledge that God is ultimately in control. He allows things to happen to us, and there is no apparent answer at the time of our trials. He does, however, sometimes give us clues later as to the why particular circumstances happened in our lives. We realize a later blessing from a particular lesson that happened to us. It happened to teach us this much-needed lesson and ultimately to bring Him glory. Other Christian authors refer to it as the providence of God, but I do believe it means much the same thing. God ultimately allows certain things to happen in believers' lives in His sovereign will.

When I find myself trying to "lean on my own understanding" and not ultimately trust in Him, this is where real perplexity enters. Along with the perplexity, a lot of human blame, anger, and resentment surfaces. A lot of things ultimately take us away from God and trusting in Him.

For almost thirty years, I did have unanswered questions as to the night my former wife died and the woman who was with her that night. It was not as clear as I would have liked in my understandings of the incident, but now those answers I once sought are no longer relevant. Ultimately, we have to accept and trust in God's providence.

I read the account of Timothy McVeigh's execution a few years ago. He was the Oklahoma City bomber who was convicted of blowing up a part of the Murrah Building, killing 168 people in 1995. Witnesses who lost loved ones, and who also witnessed his execution, claimed that there was not the closure that they had hoped for after his execution. That real closure can only come from God and trusting His providence when we lose loved ones.

We spend so much time blaming others or coming up with false blame, when we really should be trusting in God for the true answers—or no definitive answer, as in my case.

That is why the quote at the start of this chapter is so relevant. We must trust in the Lord with all our hearts and not rely on our own human understandings, even if questions remain. We should truly humble ourselves before the Lord and recognize that He is in control.

This is why Abraham trusted in the Lord, even if he did not see God's promises fulfilled in his lifetime. Abraham could not possibly envision that the Lord would do just as He promised in these verses.

> "By Myself I have sworn, says the LORD, because you have done this thing, and have not withheld your son, your only son—blessing I will bless you, and multiplying I will multiply your descendants as the stars of the heaven and as the sand which is on the seashore; and your descendants shall possess the gate of their enemies." (Genesis 22:16–17)

We must take the example from Abraham's life: he trusted in the Lord when human answers weren't as apparent as he would like. My life changed at the start of my wife's death, and change was more profound as after my son's death. If God chose to bring me closer to Him and to more fully trust Him as the result of my two loses, who am I to argue?

I was a member of my church's missionary efforts. Twelve of us went down to Peru in 2008 to help with a church that was situated in a remote village where they did not have even electricity. We had to come up with our own funding to make the trip. I decided to go, along with my teenage daughter. Worries over how I was going to pay for this endeavor were an issue, but I soon realized that God, in His sovereignty, would provide the means for us to make that trip, as He most certainly did.

We spent fifteen days down there. After getting to the village where we were to go, there were guards with AK-47s guarding a section of the road. They stopped our small minivan both coming and going. When I thought of it in my flesh, that was a huge problem. If these guards did not get the right answers to their questions as to why we wanted to pass by, or if they hated Christians, we might have all been shot because violence is a thing that is often overlooked in third-world countries. We were far away from any kind of civilization, and drugs were an issue in the area. As it turned out, through our interpreter, we could pass by with a small donation, around sixty cents after the conversion rate. The sovereignty of God had protected us right there in our encounter with the guards of this section of road, as well as throughout our trip.

Many other things that turned out to be lessons from God remain with me to this day. Certainly, the faith of these people in this village was genuine. They had so little in the way of materialistic things that we enjoy in America, yet their true joy in their faith in God is not affected by what they don't have. We ended up building pews for their church, a structure made from mud bricks. We whitewashed those mud bricks on the interior with the materials we either bought to this village or had shipped in. We also built steps to the church because it is situated on a small hill that gets very muddy and slick when it rains—and because the village is in part of the rain forest, it rains a lot there. We brought in a gas generator to power our hand tools, which we used to make the pews and the huge wooden cross that we hung in the front of the church. I remember one big, burly man from their village who decided to help us by sanding the rough mahogany boards. He took our big belt sander that we had brought in and was working up quite a sweat moving the heavy sander back and forth across the boards, which were on the seats of the partially finished pews. The light in his eyes was precious as one of us showed him how to actually turn on the sander. This man was so excited that he ended up sanding everything and wore out quite a few of our sanding belts.

I personally took along a couple of Spanish Bibles, along with a Spanish-English parallel Bible—which I picked for free at the secondhand store that I frequented in America. I gave one of the Spanish Bibles to the pastor's wife with instructions for her to distribute it to a child who was particularly needful of the Word. On the day we left, I saw the child she had selected clutching that Bible in her arms as the most precious thing she owned. Next time I go, if God directs me to go, I am going to pack less clothing and fill my suitcases with Spanish Bibles. We do take for granted our availability of the Word here in America.

Very few of us could converse in the particular form of the Spanish language they used, but it was surprising how easily we could adopt hand motions to communicate. Certain phrases like "Jesus loves you" in their form of Spanish, which I don't exactly remember now, were easily learned. The universal language of love and Jesus Christ has no language barriers.

All in all, the trip was filled with many lessons for me, especially the fact that I could trust in the sovereignty of God.

My family in America has adopted a more frugal approach to stuff that supposedly makes our lives easier. We distinguish between what is an actual luxury and what is essential. The basic thing is to be content in what you have and in not what you think you need. The writer of Hebrews certainly makes that point.

> Let your conduct be without covetousness; be content
> with such things as you have. For He Himself has said,
> "I will never leave you nor forsake you." (Hebrews 13:3)

Conclusion

Peace I leave with you, My peace I give to you; not as the world gives do I give to you. Let not your heart be troubled, neither let it be afraid. (John 14:27)

I believe my life has been one that has been filled with much testing of my faith. Certainly I could have gone through worse situations, but the main thing is I believe God has brought me through the right tests at the right time to get me to the point that I could never deny my faith, and thus I've found my way back to this peace that passes all understanding in any situation that God provides for me.

As I look back at the day my son took his life and what I witnessed, it was certainly one in which I could have gone over the edge had not Christ entered my life. It is my prayer that someone may read my book and find the hope and peace that I have found. We serve a Christ who is the way, the truth, and the life, as He claimed in John 14:6. Through that verse, we can find His peace and overcome any obstacle that comes before us.

And He said to me, "My grace is sufficient for you, for My strength is made perfect in weakness." Therefore, most gladly I will rather boast in my infirmities, that the power of Christ may rest upon me. (2 Corinthians 12:9)

This is the promise I remember whenever I face a new obstacle in life. His grace is sufficient for all situations that may come up in my life. That fact, coupled with the following verses, makes me feel I am complete.

For I am persuaded that neither death nor life, nor angels nor principalities nor powers, nor things present nor things to come, nor height nor depth, nor any other created thing, shall be able to separate us from the love of God which is in Christ Jesus our Lord. (Romans 8:38–39)

I try to remember this verse each day.

I can do all things through Christ who strengthens me. (Philippians 4:13)